Glass hummingbird

Citlali Perez

BookLeaf
Publishing

Presentation by *BookLeaf Publishing*

Web: www.bookleafpub.com

E-mail: info@bookleafpub.com

ISBN: 9789357740586

First edition 2023

DEDICATION

For my siblings that made this possible. I love you.

Goodbye letter

I just wanted to apologize to you. I am a big stupid idiot. You have always been someone that has always been there for me. You don't deserve any of those hurt feelings that I have given you. You did call me one of your closest friends and that actually struck me as I have never been called that before. I know you did mean that, and because of that I am pissed at myself for pushing you away. I was afraid to have you deal with me, but I know now you are someone who could've helped me. The fact that my dumbass did not see that really pisses me off. I know you could've changed me for the better since you were giving great advice on the flaws that I should work on. I want you to know that I am taking it seriously in changing for the better. I just hope you could give me a chance to prove to you that I do care, which is why I'm writing this letter to you. I really wish that I could've looked you straight into your eyes and asked you for help instead of running away. I am a failure for running away instead of relying on you as you have proven that you would definitely help. I want to impart this truth to you which is I really hope you could forgive me. Thank you again for being an amazing person. I am truly sorry.

Sad truth

Now I actually know. I actually know what they think of me. I hid in the car and she actually didn't see me. I meant to hide for fun, so I could scare her and it be fun for everyone. Of course she started talking about me while I was right there, completely silent and frozen. I couldn't move or do anything at first, I thought everything was good with us. The little ones were asking why she was saying that about me, but I think it's only because they knew I was there. I saw one of them look at me, so I just faked a smile like always. I didn't want them to know how I felt. I didn't want to say anything because even though she was talking about me, I would be blamed for having feelings and reacting. So yes, I just smiled like I always do.

Xihuitl

3

I want everything back to the way it was before. Now it feels like everything is falling apart and I'm alone. I know that I shouldn't tell you because you are trying to get better, but I don't want you to think I'm ignoring you.

I love you so much.

Sorrow

I'm sorry I couldn't save you. It pained me to watch you helplessly lying on the bed. I watched as the light in your eyes slowly faded away. I was only 8 at the time but I wished I would've done more. Why didn't I call for help? Why didn't I run to a neighbor's house? It haunts me to this day. You haunt me and I'm so sorry I only just sat there and watch you go. I couldn't even save me at the time, how could I ever save someone else?

Xochitl

I see the sadness in her eyes.
The confusion, the stress yet she hides it all,
swallowing her pain.
She never gives up, instead preparing to
blossom. Blossoming into a beautiful flower.
Slowly. It never happens how she expects it to.
Too slow, feeling everything that comes her way.
Finally she outgrows the old roots. Finally she is
happy.

The reflection

What's really on our mind
overthinking all the time we lose, lost her self in
doubt and now we never try.

Wondering if they're watching us and judging
every move. I feel great when it's just me and
you but the mirror never lies. I wish I could love
you like I love everyone else
I wish I could be nicer to you, but when I look at
you in the mirror there's nothing else to do, even
if I love you more than anything else no one else
would love us the same I can't look at you in the
mirror anymore. I can't handle these thoughts
anymore.
Once I look into the mirror, we are beneath
them.
Everyone is above us.
Nothing holding me back more than you.
Nothing holding me back more than looking in
the mirror. you make me feel the worst because I
can never leave you.

I'm always stuck with my reflection

Yaotyl

They say you need a mom in your life, but do I
really need mine?
My mother is the fear in my bones that shake
and rattle every time she comes close
Every time I hear the monster in her voice, every
time she drags her feet up the stairs into the
hallway.
My mother is the pain in my tears, the fall to the
floor every time words come out of her mouth.
My mother is the hurt in my heart every day and
every night. My mother is the ghost of my smile
when everything is normal.
my mother doesn't see the fear, hatred and
separation that she causes. I'm sorry if I'm not
the daughter you had in mind.
Do I really need my mother?

Trapped

Once they start, they never stop no matter how hard you try. It's always the ones you think you can trust. but once you turn around, they leave a trap and you fall right into it. They help you up like they did nothing wrong, you do believe them and keep going and after they do the same thing over and over again you finally see what is happening you act up and do it to them for the first time yet you go down instead of them once they start they don't stop

Denise

Family is family no matter what.
I didn't really know you well at all but you still
had a big impact on me.
We barely saw each other. We barely talk to each
other but once I saw you lying in the bed it all
changed.
when I saw you with no color in your skin and
no movement in your body, It felt like we talked
every day.
it felt like we were best friends like we were
even sisters.
when they were lowering you and the birds blue,
I could barely stand. I could barely see with all
the tears running down my face, dripping onto
the ground.
I barely knew you, but I love you Denise

Loves creation

That very Instance that our eyes had locked
I knew that's when it started
There was a shift in all creation,
like two worlds had collided.
       -BIG BOOM-
Sonic blast tears across the galaxy. A blinding
flash of ethereal dust and there you're standing
right in front of me.
Tried to wrap my head around it, Get a grip or
understanding.
  How can this be?
Universal mystic ways, Cosmic threads of space
and timing.

Eztli

I've always been your doll. You watched me fall
again and again. I wonder if it's going to stop.
I don't know when your strings connected to my
soul, pulling on my heart you just live to tear me
fully apart.
Out of 1000 faces I can never see you but you
never go far.
you turned my trust and loyalty into a weapon.
Your soul, part of me I'll never get back my
innocence my confidence, my pride, you took
everything I was.
you made my childhood die
you Weaponized, my insecurities, and fed on all
of my pain
how can I fight back without you showing
yourself.
You seemed so kind but I was still blind.
I still don't know who or what you are but each
face left a scar.
flashbacks memories during the day and
nightmares at night. What else do you do when
you're hurt?
how can I continue the battle of something as
miserable as a ghost?
it's hard to battle your own mind

Necalli

Waves of anxiety smash the sides of my boat,
the broken pieces fall into the empty sea
the waves are high
Then I realized I chose the destructive path.
I look around and see miles and miles of dark
black sea, which means I have to face the tide
alone again.
I try to steer the boat, but the fatal path won't get
out of my mind. My body trembles as the waves
throw me across the deck as I fall to the floor.
Once again, there is no one to help me. no one to
save me
and no one to care
I'm infected with self-hatred and have no idea
how to steer the boat away
the ship left my control hours ago and it began
to lose restraint.
The high waves began to rip the boat apart and
knock me off my feet.
I tell myself to get up to prevent the destruction,
but my stomach aches
I'm blind from flooded eyes and my mind is
controlled by the boat

These feelings inside

13

We smile we laugh we weep and we cry.
Without a mixed array of emotions.
Would we know what it is to feel alive?

Unfazed

14

As I stand there and stare back at the eyes, I
realize that there is still a part of me that is
untouched
unfazed by everything
waiting for that one day to be let out of the box
and escape. I don't know when that day will be,
but I know I will explode one day
I don't know who will make me snap or where I
will be but I will snap and it will be big
Finally that unfazed and untouched part of me,
will not be part of me anymore
when that day comes, it will be too late.
I will be someone else, and no one can help me
anymore.

Drowning

She still drowns me and kills everyone I care
about, but one person is never in the dreams I
care about. I always see my dad and siblings
dying and I get stuck alone, drowning in water.
How are you still my worst dream
I never can lose my siblings, I don't know why
you didn't want us.
I could have turned out better if I had a mom
that actually wants me
two different moms had a chance to want me
and they threw it away.
I don't want a mom anymore.
I don't need one.
I wanted one for a long time but they are not
good for me. I am not meant to have a mom.
if a great mom figure came into my life right
now, it would already be way too late.
I don't have a mom and I never will but I will
love every child that my siblings have.
I will treat them better than anyone else.
I never want to see you again.
You chose drugs over me.
I've been thrown in the trash so many times and
I still help those who were the worst to me.

My love

Be grateful for who you have, and who you love.
she's the love in my heart every day and every
night
she's the happiness in my smile, and I can talk to
her about anything anytime
she's the thoughts in my brain no matter what
even when I'm sad, making me happy.

Alone

I am in the corner too scared to open my mouth
while everyone in the room talks about me
for one tiny second I thought someone would
actually say something
my words obviously don't mean anything if
everyone acts like they can't hear one thing I say
you saw the pain in my eyes you stared at me as
if you actually cared.
You saw all the hurt I felt I know you did
but you turned around and pretended as if I
didn't exist
I will truly always be alone in this world.

Never enough

18

I can say I'm enough and I'm worth it more but I
will never believe it
I will make anyone else believe it so I can be
alone again
I can sit here and tell you the amount of times in
my life that I wasn't enough.
The times where others have told me I'm worth
nothing
my own family, friends, and strangers
I know it's true and I will never believe the
people who try and be nice.
I'm not enough, and I never will be

Nightmares

19

I have nightmares. Of us together, of us in love.
Us spending our whole lives together. We enjoy
each other's company each night I lay to rest.
Yet it's all fake.
I never loved you, and you never loved me.
Maybe it's something that I wanted deep down,
but I'm still haunted every night of what we
could've been.

Glass hummingbird

The hummingbird flew in the window trapping
itself
I reached out to help it but once I touched it, it
turned to glass and shattered.
As I cry over the glass, I realize all the
relationships I have shattered out of fear. Fear of
acceptance and love.
Maybe I should try to love more, though I'm
afraid I'll shatter another innocent soul.

Western ways

21

To be raised among these western ways is to be
bound by cold colonial shackles; whose
construct dwell wrapped around our minds
keeping the spirit up in shambles